Terms and Conditions

LEGAL NOTICE

The Publisher has strived to be as accurate and complete as possible in the creation of this report, notwithstanding the fact that he does not warrant or represent at any time that the contents within are accurate due to the rapidly changing nature of the Internet.

While all attempts have been made to verify information provided in this publication, the Publisher assumes no responsibility for errors, omissions, or contrary interpretation of the subject matter herein. Any perceived slights of specific persons, peoples, or organizations are unintentional.

In practical advice books, like anything else in life, there are no guarantees of income made. Readers are cautioned to reply on their own judgment about their individual circumstances to act accordingly.

This book is not intended for use as a source of legal, business, accounting or financial advice. All readers are advised to seek services of competent professionals in legal, business, accounting and finance fields.

You are encouraged to print this book for easy reading.

Table Of Contents

Foreword

Chapter 1:
CMS Basics

Chapter 2:
The Benefits Of CMS Web Design

Chapter 3:
Setting Up Your CMS Site

Chapter 4:
CMS And Seo

Chapter 5:
CMS And Social Branding

Chapter 6:
Integrating Analytics

Chapter 7:
Integrating E-mails

Wrapping Up

Foreword

CMS means content management system and this is a descriptive term for keeping the website up and running efficiently and smoothly. Planning a new website usually entails a lot of proper planning and thought. Therefore doing all the necessary research would definitely help to ensure all the right choices are made very early on in the exercise. Your research begins here.

CMS Connection
Using CMS To Boost Your Internet Marketing

Chapter 1:
CMS Basics

Synopsis

The focus of any website building exercise has to have a good content management system. The CMS should facilitate in assisting in the initial creation of the website and also help to serve as an administration tool that can make necessary adjustments whenever needed.

The Basics

This tool will help the website host to add, remove, and change text, graphics content and any other element that needs immediate and simple formats for change.

Using a password and username the webhost is able to access the CMS to make the administration changes in an easy and quick fashion. This is expected to be done on a timely and periodic basis as the information featured needs to be updated to give the visitor new or value added visits each time.

The CMS uses the easy administrative style that allows almost anyone who has a website to easily manipulate its contents without having any technical detailed knowledge on how the said contents is stored in the database or retrieved content.

This is because all the information that the viewer to the site is privy to comes from the database which the CMS assists in tracking both in the text and in the graphics displays chosen.

As all this information is stored electronically the webhost does not really have to worry about the various exercises that this storage process requires in terms of managing it. This tool is definitely an advantage to have especially if the webhost is not very internet savvy and does not have the time to explore all the ins and outs of the internet tools available.

Chapter 2:
The Benefits Of CMS Web Design

Synopsis

Most individuals today know and understand what they want out of their websites and how it should be designed. They are more capable of playing a proactive role in the design and content expected. This is of course very useful when there is also the assistance of a CMS tool that can further assist in the web design exercise.

Advantages

The Content management system is able to provide a number of benefits and the following are just to consider:

- The time taken to understand the various workings of a CMS program is fairly easy and does not require a lot of time. The CMS will easily facilitate the changing of data at any given time. The individual using the CMS is also able to perform simple task such as adding, changing, editing and deleting content pages.

- As all the content material and links are automatically generated in page layouts that are pre installed by the web designer it cannot be easily altered by just any content author.

- The is also the ability to keep the website up to date always and from anywhere is the world provided there is internet access. Also as all content is maintained through the web enable computer system; there is no need for additional software. This of course is a good feature as it also does not require any cost added software licensing and hardware needs.

- The designs can be changed without affecting the content and the content management functions, as designers and content managers can operate independently on the same website without disturbing each other.

Internet

Chapter 3:
Setting Up Your CMS Site

Synopsis

Setting up a CMS site is not a very difficult process but it is one that should be done with careful consideration to staying completely thorough. Focus should be given to ensuring there are no unstyled elements or half content pages on display when the site is accessed. Also the pages should be completed in a readable and interesting fashion with all the necessary draws to make it attention grabbing.

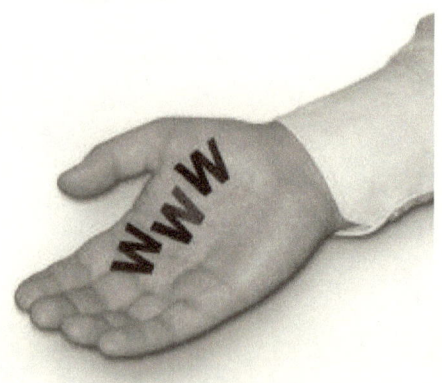

Putting It Together

The following are some points to consider when setting up a CMS site:

- Using a CMS that is based on Wordpress may be a better option to chose as this often makes the process of software sorting less of a chore.

- Opting to use a code up for the design through the HTML and CSS is also useful as a first choice as opposed to going into the CMS option at the onset. This is because it may eventually be easier to perform browse checks at the site at earlier stages and make changes and it also makes the understanding of the building platforms more manageable.

- Considering the use of Lorem Ipsum is also another good option to include as it facilitates the easier usage of coder which can be dropped into the page setup stage. This provides for all types of HTML which has already been included in the design makeup where there is a preexisting list of all the functions. That would ensure the individual is made aware of everything and whether it has been styled or not.

- Navigation is also another important element to consider including in the set up design. As the need to be constantly updating and adding on pages is definitely going to be present,

the system used should have the accommodating features to facilitate this quickly and easily. The vertical navigation may be a better option to include rather than the horizontal one which can be rather limiting at times. If there is going to be constant changes that will evolve the website then considering plug-ins is also recommended.

Chapter 4:

CMS And Seo

Synopsis

For some the CMS and SEO are inter twined and a good choice of both should entail positive advantages for any website host. However one needs to first understand the connections and capitalize on that information derived for the exercise.

Optimizing

The main target for search engine optimization is based on the good content of the website, thus by implementing a web content management system this monitoring can be correctly and advantageously done.

However this is not a firm fact to focus upon as in actual fact most CMS are not designed according to SEO marketing elements in mind, hence the following points should be carefully considered in relation to the use of both CMS and SEO.

- Bad Meta tags – Meta tags are a HTML code component that facilitates the search engine aim to evaluate the website page content. As most CMS do not have unique relevant titles or descriptions Meta tags to their content thus the search engine is unable to understand the page.

- Avoid using keyword poor URLs as this would eventually impact the search engine ranking. Keyword rich URL is a significant advantage for optimizing the possibility of improving the rankings.

- As search engines cannot really see the page, they usually base their tracking on the codes used. Most designers and CMS create pages that are mostly invisible to search engine spiders mainly because of the text images, script based navigation, overuse of AJAX and a variety of other elements. However if examined carefully these can be rectified and even avoided.

The best of both CMS and SEO elements should be explored and identified in one platform to help optimize the website. Using the advantages of the CMS to provide the relevant assistance for web designing and aligning it with the suitable promotional advantages of an SEO could be the best option to look into.

Chapter 5:
CMS And Social Branding

Synopsis

Social branding is something that should be looked into with a little knowledge and using the CMS will allow this knowledge to serve as a guild to what the individual expects to get out on the information learnt in order to facilitate an optimally run website.

Branding

Social branding is an important ingredient that is necessary for the success of the item being promoted anywhere more so in the vast arena of the internet marketing platform.

Developing the brand in which the masses will willingly support is the idea behind creating a competent social branding campaign and using the various CMS element to help make this more a manageable exercise should be considered.

The system will be able to better manage the working of the site to cater to any developments, goals, services, product launches, promotional data and any other connective information that the site generates.

It is important to have a CMS in place to ensure the webhost does not lose control of the views and intended desires of the site. Providing a certain level of culture transparency and innovation for the information featured in an easy and manageable way the CMS is a tool that should not be missed out upon.

Upon accessing platforms such customer intelligence and analysis the CMS will the assist the individual to include or tweak the information learnt to make the necessary changes to the webpage with as little complications as possible.

This can prove its merits to the individual on various levels as the ever evolving amount of information can be quite confusing to tackle

and reevaluate the web page if the assisting tools to do so are not user friendly, thus the needs for a tool like CMS. Developing and redeveloping strategies for the optimization of the website can only be done and made easier with the assistance of CMS.

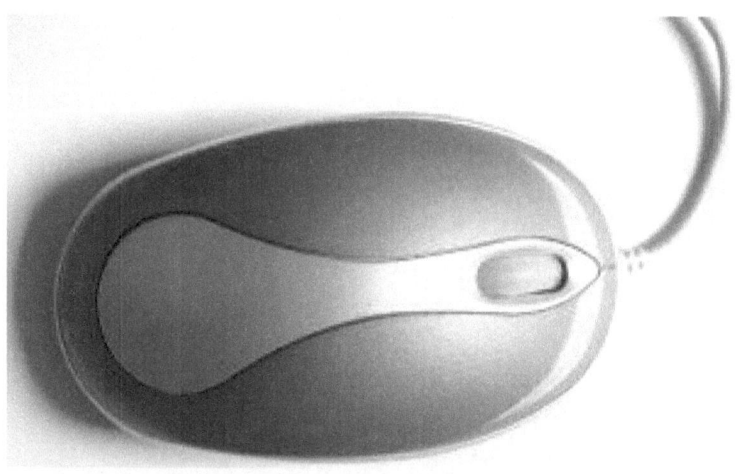

Chapter 6:
Integrating Analytics

Synopsis

The use of any tool such as various software applications that can assist in providing the means to improve on the content material of the management of any site and its ideally ever evolving site should be carefully considered for its contributing merits. This is more so when the said information needs to be constantly analyzed for its benefiting features.

The Info

These applications are usually up and running on demand and the data garnered is passed from the website into the data collection platform through the JavaScript.

This data is then processed and calculated for the key metric values where further reports are churned out on how the site is performing. However this can prove to be a problem as the analytics and CMS work on a one-way communication level which would need further connective assistance to ensure the information is managed and applied in a useful and accessible way.

The following are some points to consider in relation to integrated analytics:

Using this method the web content management can be done in a quick and efficiently systematic fashion where the metrics driven changes are made to the website on demand.

This is safe and informatively done as the information gained is from actual user reactions and perceptions of what is being viewed on the website.

This then can effectively improve the website performance and ROI, through the viewer's actions which eventually dictate the overall experience thus creating the conversion rates and generating the desired effects for success.

An accepted fact that makes the website more attractive lies in the content that drives the website usage to be optimized by visitors. Viewers will be keen to access the website for its informative value. The integration analytics and greatly assist in the content management through the continual data driven refinements.

Chapter 7:
Integrating E-mails

Synopsis

Using the many features of the CMS to further improve on the website's content is the benefits to having such an assisting tool. Designing the emails to cater to the needs of the prospects to the site can also be a tool that is managed to some level with the information gained from the CMS.

Mailing

Integration of emails as a marketing tool will provide the platform for better managements of the email campaigns within the CMS element and trigger emails that are based on promising value based on the actions derived from the site.

When the emails are designed to address the requirements of the prospects in its content value material, the impression made on the recipient of the email is an important factor to consider as it will either encourage more interaction or a total disconnect from the site.

Therefore using the information from the CMS the emails should be designed and sent out in a timely fashion in order to derive the best results possible to keep the website relevant and traffic driven.

In addition to addressing any information acquired through the various complimenting platforms and sending them out or using them to make the necessary adjustments to the website to make it more competitive, the emails can also be used to inform the prospects or visitors to the site of any impending or new developments that will be or have taken place.

When used correctly and efficiently the emails can be generated to address the following:

- The integrated system can automatically trigger targeted emails based on the information derived from the interactions with the website.

- CMS and supporting tools can automatically create emails using the content published as a guide to informing those interested in the latest developments at the site.

- Keeping in touch on a more personally designed generated email can also encourage further interaction at the website's level.

Wrapping Up

All of the CMS tools contribute to keeping the website informative, useful, and presentable and user friendly at all times, and this is a very useful objective to keep in mind when trying to stay as competitive as possible. CMS does help to eliminate the need for time consuming complicated procedures and makes your site more up to date.

We have given you the tools and knowledge to get started with this awesome tool.

www.ingramcontent.com/pod-product-compliance
Lightning Source LLC
Chambersburg PA
CBHW030602220526
45463CB00007B/3153